D1250542

It's My State!

VERMONT

The Green Mountain State

Margaret Dornfield, William McGeveran, and Steven Otfinoski

Cavendish
Square

New York

Published in 2016 by Cavendish Square Publishing, LLC
243 5th Avenue, Suite 136, New York, NY 10016

Copyright © 2016 by Cavendish Square Publishing, LLC

Third Edition

Website: cavendishsq.com

This publication represents the opinions and views of the author based on his or her personal experience, knowledge, and research. The information in this book serves as a general guide only. The author and publisher have used their best efforts in preparing this book and disclaim liability rising directly or indirectly from the use and application of this book.

CPSIA Compliance Information: Batch #WS15CSQ

All websites were available and accurate when this book was sent to press.

Library of Congress Cataloging-in-Publication Data

Otfinoski, Steven.
Vermont / Steven Otfinoski, Margaret Dornfield, and William McGeveran.
pages cm. — (It's my state!)
Includes bibliographical references and index.
ISBN 978-1-62713-181-0 (hardcover) ISBN 978-1-62713-183-4 (ebook)
1. Vermont—Juvenile literature. I. Dornfield, Margaret. II. McGeveran, William. III. Title.

F49.3.O8 2015
974.3—dc23

2015004879

Editorial Director: David McNamara
Editor: Fletcher Doyle
Copy Editor: Rebecca Rohan
Art Director: Jeffrey Talbot
Designer: Stephanie Flecha
Senior Production Manager: Jennifer Ryder-Talbot
Production Editor: Renni Johnson
Photo Research: J8 Media

The photographs in this book are used by permission and through the courtesy of: DonLand/Shutterstock.com, cover; Warren Price Photography/Shutterstock.com, Robert Shantz/Alamy, Age Fotostock/Superstock, 4; NHPA/Superstock, Bill DiLillo, University of Vermont photography/Courtesy of University of Vermont, Geology Department Perkins Museum of Geology, All Canada Photos/Superstock, 5; Michael Warwick/Shutterstock.com, 6; NHPA/Superstock, 8; Joanne Pearson/Alamy, 9; Anthony Butera/Superstock, 11; Jgorzynik/Shutterstock.com, 12; AP Photo/Toby Talbot, 13; American Spirit/Shutterstock.com, Gabe Palmer/Alamy, Magicpiano/File: Plymouth, VT Calvin Coolidge Birthplace.jpg/Wikimedia Commons, 14; Visions of America/Superstock, DonLand/Shutterstock.com, Paul Rocheleau/Photolibrary/Getty Images, 15; Visions of America/Superstock, 16; IndexStock/Superstock, 17; AP Photo/Vermont Fish & Wildlife Department, 18; AP Photo/Toby Talbot, 19; Sandy Macys/Alamy, Eric Carr/Alamy, Tom Uhlman/Alamy, 20; Science Photo Library/Alamy, Andre Jenny/Alamy, Brian Lasenby/Shutterstock.com, 21; Xprtshot/Istockphoto.com, 22; North Wind Picture Archives/Alamy, 24; Photononstop/Superstock, 25; Edward Fielding/Shutterstock.com, 27; Stock Montage/Archive Photos/Getty Images, 28; Library of Congress, 32; Rob Crandall/Alamy, Shawn Pemrick/File: Ethnic Festival 062a.jpg/Wikimedia Commons, 34; Daniel Case/File: Ritchie Block, Bennington, VT.jpg/ Wikimedia Commons, Superstock, 35; Everett Historical/Shutterstock.com, 36; AP Photo, 37; Corbis, 39; AP Photo/Toby Talbot, 40; American Spirit/Shuttestock.com, 44; AP Photo, 46; Peter Arnold Inc./Alamy, 47; North Wind Picture Archives, Scott Halleran/Getty Images, AP Photo, 48; John Bryson/The LIFE Images Collection/Getty Images, AP Photo/Al Behrman, Brian Ach/WireImage, 49; George Robinson/Alamy, 50; IndexStock/Superstock, 53; Bob Eddy/First Light Studios, Pat & Chuck Blackley/Alamy, 54; AP Photo/Jon-Pierre Lasseigne, Balfour Studios/Alamy, 55; Joe Raedle/Getty Images, 56; Age Fotostock/Superstock, 58; AP Photo/Toby Talbot, 60; AP Photo/Toby Talbot, 61; John Hoke from Albrightsville, PA/File: Howard Dean declaration of candidacy June 2003.jpg /Wikimedia Commons, AP Photo/Toby Talbot, Michael Kovac/Getty Images for The Elton John AIDS Foundation, 62; AP Photo/Toby Talbot, 63; AP Photo/Toby Talbot, 64; Farrell Grehan/Corbis, 66; Age Fotostock/Superstock, 67; Visions of America/Superstock, Lucidio Studio, Inc./Superstock, 68; H. Stanley Johnson/Superstock, IndexStock/Superstock, 69; iStock/Thinkstock.com, 70; Nik Wheeler/Alamy, 72; Dale Jorgenson/Superstock, 73; Tim Santimore/Photolibrary/Getty Images, Daniel M. Silva/Shutterstock.com, 75; Christopher Santoro, 76.

Printed in the United States of America

VERMONT ★ ★ ★ ★
CONTENTS

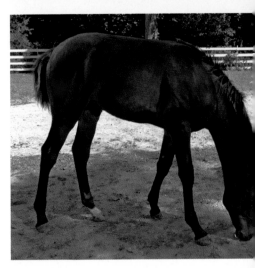

State Animal: Morgan Horse

In 1791, Justin Morgan, a teacher in West Springfield, Massachusetts, became the owner of a young stallion named Figure. The horse was small but strong and fast. Figure became the father of a new breed, the Morgan, which is still known for its athletic ability. Figure died in 1821 at age thirty-two.

State Bird: Hermit Thrush

With its brown back and speckled breast, the hermit thrush can be hard to spot in the Vermont woods. It is known for its flutelike song, which can be heard in summer from just before dawn to sunset. The hermit thrush migrates south in the winter.

State Butterfly: Monarch

In 1987, a fifth-grade class in Cornwall suggested naming the monarch as the state butterfly, and the state legislature agreed. The monarch is commonly seen in late summer and early fall. The students said its colors recall Vermont's orange autumn leaves, black soil, white snow, and yellow dandelions.

VERMONT

★ State Tree: Sugar Maple

Native Americans taught the European settlers the best way to get sap from sugar maples. Vermonters have been collecting sap—or tapping maple trees—ever since. The sap is often boiled to make syrup. It takes about 40 gallons (150 liters) of sap to make 1 gallon (3.8 l) of pure maple syrup.

★ State Fossil: White Whale

In 1849, workers building a railroad between Rutland and Burlington uncovered the fossil of a white whale in a farmer's field. It had lived some 12,500 years earlier, when waters from the Atlantic Ocean covered that low-lying region. This white whale was named the state fossil in 1993.

★ State Amphibian: Northern Leopard Frog

Northern leopard frogs, also known as meadow or grass frogs, live in Vermont's ponds and wetlands. They have spots all over their green or brown bodies. Lawmakers made the northern leopard frog a state symbol in 1998, noting that its numbers were declining.

WOODSTOCK
MIDDLE BRIDGE
1969

SLIPPERY
WHEN WET

A covered bridge in Woodstock adds
to Vermont's beautiful scenery.

The Green Mountain State

Vermont is known for its quiet woods, deep snow, and shining waters. It can bring to mind a winding road, a covered bridge, a white church, or an old-fashioned country store. But more than anything else, Vermont means mountains.

The Green Mountains run down the length of Vermont, forming a backdrop to the roadways and villages. The mountains light up with color in autumn, while in winter they cast evening shadows over snow-covered hills. They carry rivers and streams that help keep the landscape green. And they help give the state its scenic appeal. Vermont is known as the Green Mountain State, and when you travel through it, a beautiful view can be seen around every corner.

Mountains and Valleys

Vermont sits in the northeastern corner of the United States, in the region known as New England. (The other New England states are Connecticut, Maine, Massachusetts, New Hampshire, and Rhode Island.) It is the only New England state with no coastline on the Atlantic Ocean. From north to south, Vermont is about 160 miles (260 kilometers) long, and from east to west, it is 80 miles (130 km) wide on average, with a total land area of some 9,250 square miles (23,950 square kilometers). Only seven states are smaller in land

The Green Mountain National Forest runs two-thirds the length of Vermont.

Vermont Borders

North: Canada

South: Massachusetts

East: New Hampshire

West: New York

area. But it is said that if Vermont's mountains and valleys could be ironed out flat, the state would spread to the size of Texas. That would make Vermont almost thirty times bigger in land area.

The Green Mountains, Vermont's largest mountain range, run like a backbone down the center of the state. The slopes are covered with thick blankets of trees. The highest peak, Mount Mansfield, juts up 4,393 feet (1,339 meters) into the sky, making it the highest point in the state. Like other Vermont mountains, the Green Mountains were once much taller. The stone that makes up the Green Mountains has been worn down over millions of years. During the last Ice Age, which ended more than ten thousand years ago, thick sheets of slow-moving ice called **glaciers** scraped across the mountains. As the glaciers moved, they changed the shape of the land and transported huge amounts of sand, soil, and rock. Vermont still has huge rocks that the glaciers carried and left behind. One of the biggest rocks moved by a glacier is called the Green Mountain Giant. Located on a woodland trail in the southern part of the state, it is about 25 feet (8 m) high, 40 feet (12 m) long, and 125 feet (38 m) around. It is estimated to weigh some 6.8 million pounds (3 million kilograms).

The view at the top of Owl's Head Mountain in Groton rewards hikers.

Many peaks in the Green Mountains are big enough to have names. A hiking path called the Long Trail runs from one peak to another. It stretches more than 270 miles (435 km), from the top of Vermont to the Massachusetts border. Forests, waterfalls, and dazzling views mark the way.

To the east of the Green Mountains lies the Connecticut River Valley, an area of quiet towns, woods, and green rolling hills. The Connecticut River forms the border between Vermont and New Hampshire. It flows gently south toward the bottom of New England. Smaller rivers, such as the White and West Rivers, spill down the Green Mountains into the Connecticut River, rushing and swirling when the snow melts in spring.

Another valley spreads to the west of the Green Mountains. Lake Champlain is located in this valley. The lake stretches about half the length of the state, along the Vermont–New York border, a distance of about 120 miles (193 km) and as much as 12 miles (19 km) wide. Its depth averages 64 feet (20 m). It is fed in Vermont by the Missisquoi, Lamoille, and Winooski rivers, and by Otter Creek, and it drains into the Richelieu River in the Canadian province of Quebec. From there the waters eventually reach the Atlantic Ocean. Along the eastern shores of the lake, dairy cows graze on some of Vermont's richest

VERMONT
COUNTY MAP

GRAND ISLE

FRANKLIN

ORLEANS

ESSEX

LAMOILLE

CHITTENDEN

CALEDONIA

WASHINGTON

ADDISON

ORANGE

RUTLAND

WINDSOR

BENNINGTON

WINDHAM

VERMONT
POPULATION BY COUNTY

Addison	36,805
Bennington	37,076
Caledonia	31,187
Chittenden	156,763
Essex	6,297
Franklin	47,785
Grand Isle	6,958
Lamoille	24,517
Orange	28,944
Orleans	27,229
Rutland	61,573
Washington	59,558
Windham	44,504
Windsor	56,597

Source: US Bureau of the Census, 2010

Wildflowers bloom along the shore of Lake Champlain.

Champlain Bridge reconnected New York and Vermont.

farmland. The state's biggest city, Burlington, sits on the lakeshore. Thousands of people live or vacation on Lake Champlain's more than seventy islands. There are more than fifty public beaches on its shores. Some two hundred thousand people depend on Lake Champlain for their drinking water.

Lake Champlain does present a problem for Vermonters, as it provides a barrier to travel to New York. There are two bridges that cross from Vermont into New York. The Lake Champlain Bridge that connected Chimney Point, Vermont, and Crown Point, New York, was built in 1929. It was called an engineering marvel when it was built. People could travel easily between the two states. Some people could live in one state and work in the other.

The condition of the bridge got so bad in 2009 that it was closed and torn down. Engineers thought it might collapse. Closing the bridge was the safe thing to do, but it caused financial harm to Vermonters who lived and worked nearby. Their stores lost many customers from New York. Travelers had to drive around the lake, adding one hundred miles to their trip.

A group called the Lake Champlain Bridge Community complained about the loss of the bridge. It put pressure on government officials to have a new bridge built. Construction took less than two years. The new span, which is 2,200 feet (670 m) long, was opened November 7, 2011, and a celebration was held the following spring. The new bridge cost $78 million.

Climate

Vermont summers are usually mild, with warm days and cool nights. Morning mists often rise in the valleys, then dissolve into a clear blue sky. The average July temperature in Burlington is about 71 degrees Fahrenheit (22 degrees Celsius). Once in a while, a heat wave strikes. The hottest Vermont day on record was July 7, 1912, in Vernon, where the thermometer hit 107°F (42°C).

Autumn and winter can bring crisp, clear days, as well as wet weather. By January, the state is usually covered with a thick blanket of snow. Temperatures drop below freezing, and icy winds chill the air even more. Vermont winters can be long and frigid. The average January temperature in Burlington is 18°F (−8°C). The coldest recorded day was December 30, 1933, in Bloomfield, where the temperature plunged to −50°F (−46°C).

Every year, Burlington receives about 40 inches (100 centimeters) of precipitation—melted snow, rain, and other moisture. The mountainous areas in the state get the most snow—an average of around 80 to 120 inches (200 to 300 cm) each year. The Connecticut River and Lake Champlain Valleys receive less, averaging about 70 inches (180 cm) per year.

Around March, the ice and snow begin melting. But it takes weeks for spring to really arrive. Snow turns to slush, and tires sink into the muck on mountain roads. Vermonters call this period mud season. It is the one time of year many Vermonters prefer to stay inside.

Vermonters know how to make the most of winter weather.

10 KEY SITES ★ ★ ★

Ben and Jerry's Ice Cream

Bennington Battle Monument

Calvin Coolidge Birthplace

1. Ben and Jerry's Ice Cream Factory

This company, started in 1978 by two friends, is located in Waterbury. Visitors can take a tour of the factory and then visit the on-site Scoop Shop to try dozens of delicious flavors of this popular ice cream brand.

2. Bennington Battle Monument

Located in the college town of Bennington, the monument is a 306-foot (93 m) granite tower built to honor the American soldiers who defeated the invading British during the Battle of Bennington, fought in 1777.

3. Calvin Coolidge Birthplace

The thirtieth US President was born in Plymouth Notch. His homestead is a store and post office and the surrounding buildings are part of a living museum. Coolidge and his wife are buried nearby in the town cemetery.

4. Dog Chapel

This most unusual chapel in St. Johnsbury was built and designed by artist Stephen Huneck to honor man's best friend. Dogs are depicted in the pews, stained glass windows, and other features. Adjoining 150-acre (61-hectare) Dog Mountain offers plenty of walking room for dogs and their owners.

5. Grafton Village

Called one of New England's quintessential villages, Grafton boasts one of the oldest inns in America, the famed Village Cheese Factory and outlet, and an outdoor center for cross-country skiing.

6. Green Mountain National Forest

Established in 1911, Green Mountain National Forest covers a large area of central and southern Vermont. It offers visitors camping sites, many hiking trails, and scenic roads to drive through.

7. Old Constitution House

This two-story house was built in 1772 and originally served as a tavern in Windsor. The state's first **constitution** was written here in 1777. Today it is a popular state historic site.

8. Shelburne Museum

One of the largest and most unusual museums in America, the Shelburne Museum consists of more than thirty historic buildings filled with artifacts. It even houses a steamship, the *Ticonderoga*, which sailed on Lake Champlain in the nineteenth century.

9. Smugglers' Notch

This natural wonder is a wide gap between Mount Mansfield and the Sterling Mountains near the town of Stowe. During the War of 1812, smugglers brought goods through it to Boston from Canada, hence its name. Today, it is a popular ski resort.

10. Vermont Marble Museum

The museum in Proctor, part of the Vermont Marble Company, was one of the first tourist sites in the state. It features a Hall of Presidents and a multicolored Catholic chapel. A large **quarry** nearby produced stone for buildings such as the US Supreme Court.

Old Constitution House

OLD CONSTITUTION HOUSE 1777

Smugglers' Notch

Vermont Marble Museum

There is beauty around every turn in the road in Vermont.

Forests and Fields

Large areas of Vermont's forests were once cleared for farming, and by the late 1800s, only 20 to 30 percent of the land was forested. Although the woods have grown back, the remains of stone walls from old farms can still be seen among the trees.

Outside the Lake Champlain Valley, the state today is carpeted with woods, broken up by ribbons of roads and patches of farm fields and villages. In all, more than three-quarters of the land is wooded. There are more than one hundred kinds of trees in the forests. Evergreens include spruce, fir, hemlock, and cedar trees. Beside them grow **deciduous** trees, which lose their leaves in the fall. These include maples and birches, along with ash, elm, beech, hickory, and poplars.

When autumn comes, it sets the woods glowing with brilliant colors. Beeches, ashes, and hickories turn different shades of yellow. Sugar maples turn amber, gold, and scarlet. Vermont's fall leaves are so bright that tourists come from other states and even foreign countries to see the display. The amount of color varies from year to year, depending on weather conditions. Sunny fall days with cool nights help the leaves turn brightest. Fall color reports in newspapers and on the Internet—a little like weather reports—help "leaf peepers" (people on the lookout for brightly colored fall leaves) hit the best spots at the right times.

In winter months, the maples and other deciduous trees are bare and trimmed with snow. But just before the first buds of spring appear, the sap of sugar maples starts flowing. Vermonters tap them around this time and boil down the sweet liquid to produce maple syrup.

Biggest Lake

While Lake Champlain is the largest lake in New England, Lake Bomoseen, which is west of Rutland, is the largest lake that is entirely in Vermont.

In spring and summer, delicate wildflowers bloom in the Vermont woods. White, yellow, and purple violets cluster between the roots of trees. Irises grow on the banks of streams, and bog laurel crowds mountain marshes. In September, goldenrods and purple asters fill Vermont meadows.

Running Wild

The Vermont woods are rich in wildlife. Chipmunks dart between rocks, around trees, and over logs. These and many other forest animals lie low during much of the day and are most active around late afternoon or evening. White-tailed deer may nibble green twigs at sunset, and moose wade through rivers in the northeast woods. Beavers swim out from their lodges to chew on aspen trees. Rabbits leave their burrows to look for food. So do **predators** such as bobcats, minks, and foxes. Bears are also most active around twilight.

Beavers help change the face of Vermont's wooded landscape.

The cool lakes and rivers of the Green Mountain State are filled with fish. Big fish, such as landlocked salmon and northern pike, and small ones, such as smelt, share the deep waters of Lake Champlain. Perch, trout, and bass are among the many kinds of fish that live in rivers and streams. Many birds that live near the water, such as herons, egrets, kingfishers, and osprey, depend on the fish for food.

Two hundred years ago, the North American cougar—also called the puma, mountain lion, catamount, or panther—roamed the Green Mountains. This big cat, with its wild grace, once stood for the freedom of the Vermont frontier. But farmers and loggers cleared acres of forests, destroying the cougar's natural habitat. Hunters and trappers killed animals the big cats needed for food, as well as the cats themselves. Vermont's last known cougar was killed in 1881.

In fact, cougars have died out in most of the eastern United States. They are now listed by the federal government as an endangered species. In recent decades, hundreds of people have reported seeing cougars in Vermont, but so far there has been no confirmation that cougars are back. If the big cats ever did make a comeback, the remote woods in the northern part of the state would be a likely place for them.

Cleaning Up

Vermont is a leading state when it comes to protecting the environment and endangered species; that is, animals or plants that are in danger of becoming extinct. The little brown bat has been dying in record numbers from a mysterious disease known as white-nose syndrome. The disease affects hibernating bats. It had killed 90 percent of cave bats in the northeast as of the fall of 2014. Scientists are working on ways to stop the white fungus that grows on the muzzles and wings of bats and seems to cause their deaths. The drop in the bat population is a serious threat to the Vermont **economy**. Bats eat many insects. Some of these insects are the kind that can damage crops. By eating them, bats save farmers from billions of dollars in crop losses and they reduce the amounts of pesticides that are used.

Outdoorsmen benefit from laws that protect Vermont's environment. *BIG FISHERMAN*

Jesup's milk-vetch is an endangered plant that is in danger of completely dying out. People are not allowed to pick it, even if they own the land it grows on.

Another environmental challenge Vermonters face is keeping their water healthy. Lakes and ponds are especially threatened by phosphorus, a chemical that gets washed from farms, cities, and sewage treatment plants into the state's waterways. As phosphorus builds up in lakes, it causes too much **algae** to grow. As the algae rapidly spreads, it can rob other plants and animals of needed oxygen until they sicken and die. One spot where algae has become a serious problem is Missisquoi Bay, in northern Lake Champlain.

Vermont citizens have helped the state monitor algae and phosphorus levels at different spots in Lake Champlain. This research gives scientists a rough idea of how much phosphorus is too much. In 2003, the state government announced its initial plans to deal with these and other environmental problems affecting Lake Champlain, and in 2010, the state of Vermont, along with New York State and the Canadian province of Quebec, agreed to a joint long-term management plan for the lake. It was aimed in part at reducing phosphorus levels, preventing contamination by toxic substances, and managing species that threaten the lake's ecosystem.

Scientists test samples of Vermont's water to make sure it stays clean.

Black Bear

Chickadee

Little Brown Bat

1. Black Bear

Black bears are the only bears in Vermont. Though smaller than other types of bears, black bears are still large. An adult male usually weighs around 300 to 400 pounds (140 to 180 kg). Vermont is believed to be home to more than three thousand black bears.

2. Chickadee

Black-capped chickadees live in Vermont all through the year. They often form small flocks and hop between branches of evergreen trees. When threatened by an intruder, a chickadee warns other birds with its familiar call of "chick-a-dee-dee-dee."

3. Goldenrod

One of Vermont's most common wild flowers, goldenrod has a thin stem and clusters of bright yellow flowers. It can be dried for floral decorations, or its leaves can be used to brew tea. Its leaves also produce an oil that has medicinal use as a tonic.

4. Jesup's Milk-Vetch

Jesup's milk-vetch grows in only a few places in the United States. A member of the pea family, it has bluish-purple flowers. It clings to the thin soil on rocks along the Connecticut River near Hartland.

5. Little Brown Bat

The most common of the state's nine bat species, these mammals live in barns and attics in warm weather and in caves and old mines during the winter. They can eat half their body weight in insects each night.

6. Red Clover

The red clover, which is often seen along Vermont's country roads, was named the state flower in 1894. Farmers grow red clover to help fertilize their fields and to provide feed for cows and other farm animals.

7. Red Maple

The red maple is one of the jewels of the Vermont woods. It shows red buds in winter, red flowers in spring, and red leaf stems in summer. But it truly stands out in early fall, when its leaves turn an especially fiery red.

8. Snowshoe Hare

On winter mornings, the Vermont woods are often crisscrossed with the tracks of snowshoe hares. These animals change color with the seasons. In early fall, they gradually replace their brown coats with white fur to match the winter snow.

9. Spring Peeper

The tiny frogs called spring peepers are easier to hear than they are to see. They perch on the grasses that grow near ponds and wetlands and loudly peep to find mates in spring.

10. Wild Turkey

In the 1800s, Vermonters cleared so much land that many woodland animals, including the wild turkey, died out. But about forty years ago, biologists brought some wild turkeys back to Vermont. Their population increased rapidly, and wild turkeys now nest again in the Green Mountains.

Red Clover

Snowshoe Hare

Spring Peeper

Vermont's history is tied to Lake Champlain and its surroundings, including Fort Ticonderoga.

From the Beginning

More than ten thousand years ago, when the glaciers melted at the end of the last Ice Age, people called Paleo-Indians began moving into the land that is now Vermont. At the time, there were wide stretches of mostly open land. This land looked like the tundra in today's Arctic regions of the world. The weight of the glaciers had lowered the level of some of the land, creating a huge valley. Water from the ocean flowed into this valley and formed a big sea.

The Paleo-Indians probably camped in small groups along the shores of this saltwater sea. They may have caught fish, seals, and shellfish to eat. They may also have hunted the caribou that once roamed the land in gigantic herds. No one knows exactly what life was like for these early people. The only clues that have been found are spear tips and other stone tools.

Over the centuries, the climate got warmer, and the landscape slowly changed. The land, crushed down by glaciers, gradually rose back up. The saltwater sea dried up, and eventually a smaller freshwater lake, now known as Lake Champlain, was formed. Forests spread across the hills.

In time, the people learned to make pottery from clay. They still hunted and fished, and they also gathered food, such as acorns, hickory nuts, and raspberries, from the forest. Eventually, they learned to grow crops such as beans, squash, and corn.

At the time European explorers first arrived in the region, villages dotted the shores of Lake Champlain and the Connecticut River. The villages belonged to a Native American group called the Abenaki. The original five tribes of the Iroquois, or "The People of the Longhouse," lived in large numbers to the west of the lake, in an area that is now part of New York State. They visited and at times lived in parts of what is now Vermont, and they became enemies of the Abenaki.

Newcomers Arrive

In July 1609, a group of Native American warriors from the Quebec region paddled into the great lake the Abenaki called Bitawbagok. With them were Samuel de Champlain, the French explorer and founding father of Quebec, and two other white companions.

"We entered the lake, which is of great extent, say eighty or a hundred leagues long, where I saw four fine islands …" wrote Champlain in his journal upon seeing the lake. "There are also many rivers falling into the lake, bordered by many fine trees."

The group came face-to-face with a number of Iroquois. (The Iroquois were longtime enemies of the northern Native Americans accompanying the French.) Champlain fired his gun, killing two Iroquois leaders. In the battle that followed, the Iroquois, armed only with bows and arrows, were easily defeated. Many fled in fear of the strange men with powerful weapons. Champlain named the lake after himself and claimed the land around it for France. As far as anyone knows, he and his men were the first Europeans to see the lake.

Samuel de Champlain's first encounter with the Iroquois resulted in a victory.

Native guides led Samuel de Champlain to the lake that bears his name. He claimed the area for France.

The Abenaki were not a part of this battle, and they never met Champlain. But they saw many changes soon after his arrival. More Frenchmen followed in Champlain's footsteps. They acquired furs from the Abenaki in return for cotton cloth, iron pots, glass beads, and other goods new to the Abenaki. The French wanted a good relationship with the Abenaki and supplied them with guns and ammunition that could help them fight their enemies.

In 1666, a French captain named Pierre La Motte, sent by King Louis XIV, built a fort in the wilderness on an island in Lake Champlain (an island later named after La Motte). The fort, named Saint Anne, protected French territory from attack. Fort Saint Anne was the first European settlement in what is now Vermont. Other French forts and villages sprang up along the lakeshore. On the other side of the Green Mountains, in 1724, British soldiers of the Massachusetts **militia** built Fort Dummer as a frontier defense against French and Native American forces. This fort, on the Connecticut River, opened up permanent settlement by British colonists in what is now southeastern Vermont.

As Europeans pushed in from both sides, clashes broke out. The Native Americans, except for the Iroquois, mostly sided with the French. In the French and Indian War, which began in 1754, the Abenaki helped capture more than a thousand British settlers. They marched their prisoners north through present-day Vermont to lands controlled by France. Some prisoners died on the way, but many lived to tell their stories. They painted a vivid picture of the Native Americans and the wild country they had traveled through.

The Native People

There were five major Native American tribes living in the area of Vermont at the time Europeans first arrived. They were the Abenaki, Mohican, Missiassik, Pennacook, and Pocomtuc. Most of them were sub tribes of the Algonquian family. The Iroquois family of tribes from New York drove most of these tribes out of the region. However, the French colonists, who were enemies of the warlike Iroquois, helped the Algonquians defeat them, and they were able to reclaim Vermont.

These native peoples had a common Algonquian heritage, culture, and language. They were a nomadic people for many years, traveling between the Connecticut River and Lake Champlain. They lived by gathering food, farming, hunting, and fishing. The Abenaki were originally inhabitants of Vermont, New Hampshire and Maine. They were part of an organization called the Wabanaki Confederacy along with neighboring tribes, including the Penobscot, the Maliseet, the Passamaquoddy, and the Mikmak.

Both the English and French settlers brought diseases like tuberculosis, measles, smallpox, cholera, and influenza to which the native peoples had no resistance or immunity. They died off in large numbers. Their numbers rose, however, in 1676 when thousands of refugees from southern New England tribes joined them, fleeing from King Philip's War, a struggle between native peoples and English colonists in Connecticut and Massachusetts. However, the Abenaki and other tribes never regained their power or influence and lost most of their land to the English.

Today Native Americans make up a very small proportion of the population. After years of struggle for recognition, four tribes are now recognized by the state – the Elnu Abenaki, Nulhegan Abenaki, Koasek Traditional Band of the Koas Abenaki Nation, and the Abenaki Nation at Missisquoi. None of these have yet received federal recognition. The Vermont Commission on Native American Affairs (VCNAA) protects and assists in the heritage of these tribes and helps to meet their needs.

Spotlight on the Abenaki

The word "Abenaki" is derived from *Wabanaki*, which means "people of the dawn."

Shelter: The Abenaki lived in **wigwams**, which is a word they invented, made of wooden frames that were covered with wide strips of bark from birch, basswood, or elm trees. They also used birch bark for canoes and baskets.

The Abenaki covered their wigwams with bark from birch trees.

Food: The lives of the Abenaki changed with the seasons. In winter, they paddled upstream to the mountains to hunt moose and deer. When spring was on its way, they collected sap from sugar maple trees to make maple syrup. In summer and fall, they tended their fields and gathered wild plants to make medicine. They dried meat, fish, berries, and corn to eat when the weather turned cold.

Clothing: The men wore breechcloths with leather leggings. The women wore deerskin skirts. Both wore moccasins on their feet and billowy blouses and cloaks in cold weather.

Art: The arts were important to the Abenaki. They enjoyed storytelling, music, basketmaking, and beadwork. They also practiced traditional medicine, making healing potions from herbs and other plants.

Life Today: After the colonists arrived, many Abenaki fled to Canada, where they still live today on two reservations in Quebec. Most of the Abenaki in this area speak French. Other tribe members live across New England, but because the tribe is not recognized officially in the United States it has no reservation.

The Abenaki people, however, were under pressure from expanding British settlements. Most of them moved north toward present-day Canada, leaving lands their ancestors had occupied for centuries. The French suffered key defeats in the region, including the loss of Fort Ticonderoga in New York, on the western shore near the southern end of Lake Champlain. In 1763, the French signed a peace treaty, ending the war.

The Green Mountain Boys

With the treaty of 1763, the British won control of virtually all of eastern North America. Even before then, British settlers were clearing new land. The royal governor of New Hampshire, Benning Wentworth, sold many pieces of land—known as grants—in the area just to the west of the Green Mountains. By 1770, hundreds of people from Massachusetts and Connecticut owned, or believed they owned, these lands.

Wentworth claimed that this land was owned by the New Hampshire colony. However, in the eyes of the British government, it belonged to the colony of New York. New York officials tried to make the land-grant settlers leave or pay rent on their farms. Most of them refused, and they teamed up to defend their property.

In an engraving of a painting by Alonzo Chappel, Ethan Allen surprises British Captain William Delaplace to capture Fort Ticonderoga.

Their leader, a settler named Ethan Allen, went to a court in Albany, New York, to plead their case. But the court rejected his argument. According to one account, he reacted with a remark that is now famous among Vermonters: "The gods of the hills are not the gods of the valley." In other words, he believed that New Yorkers would lose out in the end.

After the court decision, in 1770, Allen gathered about two hundred men to fight for the New Hampshire grants. They called themselves the Green Mountain Boys. Instead of wearing uniforms, they wore evergreen twigs in their caps. They harassed and sought to drive away settlers who sided with New York by stealing cattle, burning buildings, and sometimes carrying out floggings. They stopped sheriffs who were trying to enforce the laws of New York.

A Daring Attack

Ethan Allen's attack on Fort Ticonderoga was made at night. All eighty-three British soldiers, including the sentry at the open gate and two officers, were asleep and taken completely by surprise. The fort was surrendered without a shot being fired.

A New Republic

At first, New Yorkers called the Green Mountain Boys "rioters and traitors." But when the colonies began fighting for independence from Great Britain, this militia was an important part of the patriot cause. In May 1775, soon after the first shots of the American Revolution had been fired, the Green Mountain Boys, led by Ethan Allen and Seth Warner, captured Fort Ticonderoga from the British. No one was killed in the surprise attack. The Green Mountain Boys next captured Crown Point, the other fort on Lake Champlain, and took a British warship. When New York leaders found out, they actually paid the men and bought them uniforms.

Capturing Fort Ticonderoga was important for the Continental Army because there were one hundred cannons and other weapons stored there. The patriot forces did not have many cannons because those weapons were controlled by the British army. The weapons taken from the fort were moved across Vermont to Dorchester Heights above Boston. They were used to end the siege of Boston. The British, who were occupying the city, left it.

Most settlers in the New Hampshire grants believed in the American Revolution. But they did not want their territory to be part of New York. So in January 1777, at a meeting in the town of Westminster, leaders in the region proclaimed it to be "a separate and independent state, or government." It was later named the Republic of Vermont, based on the French words *vert mont*, which mean "green mountain."

Making a Vermont Village

Vermont is known for its tidy, small villages. You can make your own Vermont village out of food boxes and paper towel tubes. Just follow the instructions below.

What You Need

Various sized empty food boxes (cereal, crackers, pasta)

Paper towel tubes

Graph paper

Cellophane tape

Scissors

Green construction paper

Metal brads

What to Do

- Wrap graph paper around each box and seal it with tape. These will be your buildings.

- Cut a small rectangle of construction paper of a different color and press a brad through it to attach it the building. This will be a door.

- Cut a corner off another box to make a triangle and wrap it in paper. Place it on top of the building as a roof. Press a wad of crumpled green construction paper into each paper towel tube to make a tree. Arrange your houses and trees in a group to form a village.

- You might want to add toy figures as people and model cars to complete your Vermont village.

In July 1777, Vermont leaders gathered at a tavern in the town of Windsor to adopt a constitution for their independent republic. It was the first such constitution to outlaw slavery. In addition, the Vermont constitution was the first to authorize a system of public schools.

In 1778, Vermonters elected a group of representatives called the Vermont Assembly. Vermonters wanted their "republic" to be represented in the Continental Congress formed by the American colonies now fighting for their independence. However, because of New York's opposition, this did not happen.

Earlier, the Vermonters had built a fort on the eastern side of Lake Champlain, opposite Fort Ticonderoga. They were forced to abandon it when a British force of seven thousand men moved into the area from Canada. But in August 1777, the Green Mountain Boys, now led by Seth Warner, joined forces with patriot troops, and together they defeated the British in the so-called Battle of Bennington. (It was actually fought in what is now New York state, near Bennington.) A few months later, the British were defeated at Saratoga, New York. This was the last battle fought in or near Vermont during the American Revolution, but the British and their Native American allies raided towns in Vermont throughout the war. On October 16, 1780, a British regiment, joined by some three hundred Iroquois, raided the town of Royalton and many homesteads along Vermont's White River. They burned houses and barns and slaughtered livestock. They killed four Americans and captured twenty-seven others, who were taken back to Canada.

The Fourteenth State

The American Revolution ended with a treaty signed in Paris in 1783. Under this treaty, the British finally recognized American independence. With the country at peace, Vermont's population climbed. By 1785, Vermont had its own newspaper and post offices. The tiny republic even issued its own copper coins.

In 1790, New York and Vermont finally came to an agreement. Vermont promised to pay New York $30,000 to put old arguments to rest. In 1791, the Vermont Assembly voted 105 to 2 to adopt the US Constitution. That same year, every member of the US Congress voted to accept Vermont as the fourteenth state. Thomas Chittenden, who had been governor of the Vermont republic, was elected as the first governor of the new state.

Vermont had about eighty-five thousand residents when it joined the Union—almost three times as many as when the republic was formed. Over the next twenty years, it became the nation's fastest-growing state. New settlers cleared land for farming. They built sawmills along streams and dug canals to help boats carry goods between towns.

The settlers did not have an easy life. Farming the rocky soil of the Green Mountains was backbreaking work. Some years, heavy rainstorms made streams overflow and wash away bridges and barns. In other years, there was almost no rain at all.

Independent Thinking

Vermonters began showing their independent spirit early on. In 1798, President John Adams signed into law the Alien and Sedition Acts. The law was written because of threats to the new United States from France. It was aimed at foreigners. However, it also restricted freedom of the press and forms of protest against the government. The law also made it easier to deport **immigrants** and made it harder for immigrants to vote.

A Vermonter named Matthew Lyon was one of the first people arrested under these acts. Lyon was born in Ireland and joined the Green Mountain Boys after moving to the area that would become Vermont. He became a successful businessman and was elected to the House of Representatives in 1797 on his third try. He was a Republican. The Alien and Sedition Act was passed by the Federalists, a political party that no longer exists.

A cartoon shows the fight between Vermonter Matthew Lyon (tongs) and Roger Griswold at Independence Hall in 1798.

The fiery Lyon established a newspaper and used it to criticized members of the Federalist Party, including the president. On February 15, 1798, Connecticut Representative Roger Griswold attacked Lyon because he felt the criticism had become personal. Griswold hit Lyon with his walking stick while they were in the House chamber. Lyon picked up fireplace tongs in defense and a brawl broke out.

Lyon was one of twenty newspaper editors arrested under the act. He pleaded not guilty and said the Alien and Sedition Acts were not constitutional. He was convicted of defaming the president and sent to jail for four months and fined $1,000. While he was in prison, he ran for reelection and won. The Federalists called Lyon the "Beast of Vermont." However, the Alien and Sedition Acts were unpopular. Some of the acts were repealed in 1802 and the rest expired, so they are no longer the law.

It was clear Lyon was unjustly prosecuted. In 1840, Congress repaid Lyon's $1,000 fine plus interest to his heirs.

Emma Willard was another independent thinker who lived in Vermont. She started teaching scientific and classical subjects to women in her home in Middlebury in 1814. She did this because of the big difference in the level of education given to women compared to the level given to men. Her ideas on improving women's education got the approval of many people including of two former presidents, Thomas Jefferson and John Adams, in 1819. Then she was asked to open a school in New York. The Emma Willard School is still educating young women in Troy, New York.

Building a Future

Many Vermonters opposed the War of 1812, a conflict between the United States and Great Britain. The conflict started because the British and the French under Napoleon were at war and wanted to block their enemies from trading with the United States. The Royal Navy often captured US merchant ships, and forced the sailors to fight for them.

The Vermonters did not want the war to disrupt the state's trade with Canada, which was then still a British possession. However, patriotic volunteers from Vermont went to New York to help defend the town of Plattsburgh in September 1814, near the end of the war.

Vermonters started raising a lot of sheep during the War of 1812, when the country needed wool. By 1840, Vermont had six times as many sheep as people. In the 1850s, however, when sheep farming spread to the wide open spaces farther west, the industry declined in Vermont.

Times were difficult after the war ended in 1815. Cheap goods from Britain became available, forcing many Vermonters out of business. Manufacturing jobs were in short

★ 10 KEY CITIES ★ ★ ★

Burlington

Rutland

1. Burlington: population 42,417

Burlington is located in the northwest part of the state on Lake Champlain. It is a busy port, an industrial center, and the home of the main campus of the University of Vermont. Battery Park was the scene of a British naval attack during the War of 1812.

2. Essex: population 19,587

Essex is located in northwest Vermont on the Winooski River. Nearby is historic Fort Ethan Allen, a cavalry outpost built in 1894. Essex is home of the annual Champlain Valley Exposition.

3. South Burlington: population 17,904

South Burlington is a major suburban area of Burlington. It is home to CommutAir, a regional airline, and Magic Hat Brewing Company, one of the nation's largest craft beer breweries. It also boasts the state's largest enclosed shopping mall, the University Mall.

4. Colchester: population 17,067

Colchester is another suburb of Burlington, and lies just north of it. It is the home of the annual Lake Champlain International Father's Day Fishing Derby.

5. Rutland: population 16,495

Rutland is in central Vermont at the junction of Otter and East Creeks. It is famous for its marble quarries and the ski resorts that surround it. Rutland is also headquarters of the Green Mountain National Forest. A state fair is held here yearly.

6. Bennington: population 15,764

This historic town consists of two villages, North Bennington and Old Bennington. It is home to Bennington College and the first schoolhouse in Vermont.

7. Brattleboro: population 12,046

Brattleboro is located in southeastern Vermont on the Connecticut River. It is a manufacturing center and hub for winter sports, especially skiing. Brattleboro was once an artists' colony. Author Rudyard Kipling's wife was a local woman and the couple lived nearby for several years.

8. Milton: population 10,352

Legend has it that Milton is named in honor of English poet John Milton, but it is probably named for an English Viscount. Located in northwest Vermont, Milton's most famous son is nineteenth century clergyman and teacher George Allen.

9. Hartford: population 9,952

Hartford lies on the New Hampshire border in eastern Vermont. If is made up of five villages and was named for Hartford, Connecticut. Horace Wells, a dentist who was an early supporter of anesthesia, was from Hartford.

10. Springfield: population 9,373

Springfield, in southeast Vermont, is known for its machine-tool industry started more than a century ago by noted inventor and businessman James Hartness. It is also the center of a thriving fruit and dairy farming region.

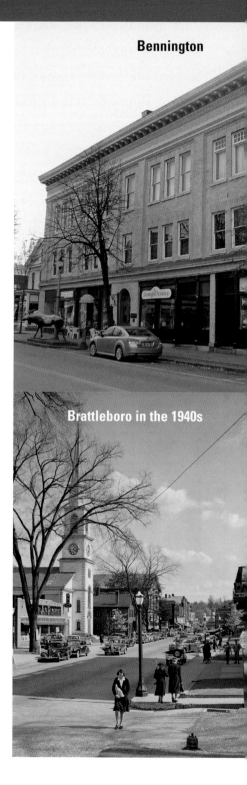

Bennington

Brattleboro in the 1940s

supply. A long-lasting frost in 1816 destroyed crops. This was the "year without a summer," when many people in the United States and Europe died of starvation due to the failure of their crops. The cold, wet weather that summer was blamed on the eruption of the volcano on Mount Tambora in Indonesia. So much material was sent into the atmosphere that it blocked the sun and caused climate change. Many farmers moved farther west, where land was better and more plentiful.

As the nation grappled with the issue of slavery in the mid-1800s, Vermonters became involved. They had already outlawed slavery in their state. The first article of Vermont's constitution states that "all persons are born equally free and independent," and that no one may be bound as a servant, slave, or apprentice without their consent.

Thomas Mcdonough's crew helps turn the tide of the War of 1812 by winning the Battle of Plattsburg on Lake Champlain in September 1814.

Michael Middleton painted *13th Vermont Regiment at Gettysburg* to show the volunteer troops fighting against Pickett's Charge.

They now promoted efforts to move free blacks back to Africa. They also sheltered escaped slaves from the South who were traveling north to Canada along a secret route called the Underground Railroad. The "railroad" was a network of homes, churches, and other places where escaped slaves could rest and receive food and other needed supplies as they journeyed north. The first safe house for slaves in Vermont was at a farm in Shaftsbury. Escaped slaves stayed there in June 1843. The best known site in the state is Rokeby, the well preserved farm in Ferrisburgh that belonged to the Rowland Thomas Robinson family. So strong was Vermont's opposition to slavery that Harriet Beecher Stowe made a New England character in *Uncle Tom's Cabin* a Vermonter. The book was anti-slavery and tried to humanize the African Americans who suffered under slavery.

Vermont also passed laws to keep slave owners from capturing escaped slaves in the state and taking them back. This ran against the Fugitive Slave Act passed by Congress in 1850. Many people in Vermont gave jobs to escaped slaves and helped them to start new lives.

In 1861, the Civil War broke out between the North and South. Vermont was the first state to offer troops to the North. About thirty-five thousand Vermont men fought in the war, and some ten thousand were killed or disabled. The Civil War touched Vermont territory in October 1864. Twenty-one Confederate horsemen came down from Canada and tried to take over the town of St. Albans in the state's northwest. They robbed three banks and attempted to set the town on fire, but they ended up burning only a woodshed. By the time they were driven away, one town resident had been killed and one of the raiders had been fatally wounded. The rebels fled to Canada with $20,000 they had stolen.

Progressive Party

Vermonters have a reputation for voting independently. In 1832, they gave their presidential electoral votes to third party candidate William Wirt of the Anti-Masonic Party. This long-forgotten political party was the first to have a nominating convention and adopt a national platform in its campaigns.

After the war ended in 1865 with a Northern victory, slavery was abolished nationwide.

In the years following the Civil War, **agriculture** continued to decline in Vermont. Many people left to try their luck in other parts of the country. Some Vermonters who stayed on earned their living raising dairy cows. The state's dairy farms became famous for their milk, cheese, and butter. Other people found work in Burlington lumber mills. Still others worked in factories making machine tools. And once railroads had been built to help transport heavy goods, Vermont became a leading source for granite and marble used nationwide.

Some Vermont businesses brought in workers from other parts of the world. Scottish, Spanish, and Italian immigrants cut and carved granite in Barre. People from Poland, Spain, Greece, and Russia worked for the Vermont Marble Company in Proctor.

New Vermont

In both World War I (1914–1918) and World War II (1939–1945), Vermont's industries supplied clothing, machine tools, lumber, and other goods to help the war efforts. Some sixteen thousand Vermonters served in the armed forces in World War I, which the United States entered in 1917, and about forty thousand served in World War II, which the United States entered in 1941.

Two Vermont natives have become president of the United States. Chester A. Arthur, born in 1829 in Fairfield, was elected vice president in 1880 and became president after

The flood of 1927 devastated the streets of Montpelier.

James Garfield was assassinated in 1881. He signed a law aimed at awarding government jobs and promotions on the basis of merit.

Calvin Coolidge, born in 1872 in Plymouth Notch, was elected vice president in 1920 and became president in 1923, after President Warren G. Harding died in office. Known for his strong pro-business views, "Silent Cal" was a man of few words. He was elected to a full term in 1924 but did not run for a second full term, saying only, "I do not choose to run for president in 1928."

In 1927, a severe flood caused mainly by a fall of heavy rain destroyed miles of roads, 1,285 bridges, and thousands of homes in Vermont. It killed eighty-five people and left nine thousand homeless. In the Great Depression of the 1930s, a time of severe economic hardship nationwide, some fifty thousand Vermonters lost their jobs. There were only 360,000 people living in the state in 1930, so the job loss totaled almost 14 percent of the population. The Civilian Conservation Corps, created by President Franklin D. Roosevelt, put many back to work. Workers built state parks, highways, and other facilities, including a number of dams intended to prevent a repeat of the 1927 flood disaster.

During the late 1800s, the state had begun to attract summer visitors, who were eager for the chance to hunt, fish, or experience country life on a farm. But it was not until the 1930s that Vermonters learned to make the most of their steep slopes and winter snowstorms. When Americans took up skiing, Vermonters realized they had "white gold." The first ski lift in the United States was built in Woodstock in 1934. The simple towrope that took skiers to the top of the slope got its power from the engine of a Ford Model T automobile. Six years later, the nation's first chairlift started carrying skiers in Stowe.

Vermont became known as a vacation spot thanks to the ski season. Many skiers came back in summer and fell in love with the quiet, unspoiled land. And a major road-building program in the late 1950s helped open up the state to greater numbers of visitors.

State residents strongly protested against the Vermont Yankee nuclear power plant.

Women began to become a power in the state by the 1950s. In 1952, fifty-two women were elected to the Vermont House of Representatives. Three years later, Consuelo Northrop Bailey became the first woman elected Speaker of the Vermont House. Liberal ideas began to change the landscape of Vermont politics. Third political parties such as the Libertarian Party and Liberty Union gained widespread support. In 1982, Bernie Sanders was elected the first Socialist mayor of Burlington.

By the 1960s, people who wanted to escape from the cities found Vermont a great place to start new lives. Some young men and women who wanted to get closer to nature began small farms in Vermont. Vacation houses popped up in the mountains and around lakes. Many writers and artists also relocated. Today, Vermont has about two-thirds more people than it did in the 1950s. The state has more buildings, more traffic, and more roads as well. But it also has more laws and programs to protect Vermont's environment and **rural** character.

Independent Ideas

In 1968, a grassroots effort spurred lawmakers to pass a measure banning all billboards on Vermont highways. In 1970, **legislators** passed the Environmental Control Law, also known as Act 250, which allows the state to limit development based on its impact on the environment. Also in 1970, the state government launched Vermont's first Green Up Day. The event, now organized by a private nonprofit company, is held every year on the first Saturday in May. Vermont children take the day to clean up litter in parks and along roadways and waterways throughout the state. These and other steps have helped preserve the state's natural beauty.

Vermont's first nuclear power plant, Vermont Yankee, opened in 1972 in Vernon, along the Connecticut River. By 2008, the plant was providing 35 percent of the state's total electricity needs. Despite this, the plant was controversial from the start and generated many public protests over its safety. The plant closed in 2014 because it was losing money. Residents in Vernon and other communities support it being replaced by a gas-fired power plant.

In 1986, the federal government's Whole Herd Buyout program had a negative effect on Vermont farming. The program was meant to reduce the supply of milk in order to raise prices to a fair level. That year, 350 state farms went out of business, some 192 of them supposedly as a result of the buyout. Some farms remained in business by raising beef cows or even such exotic animals as emus and llamas.

Vermont continued to display its political independence in the twenty-first century. Senator James Jeffords left the Republican Party in 2001 and declared himself an independent. Subsequently, the Democratic Party gained control of the Senate for the first time since 1994. The previous year (2000), the Vermont General Assembly passed a controversial law granting rights of marriage to same sex couples in civil unions.

In Their Own Words

"I love Vermont because of her hills and valleys, her scenery and invigorating climate, but most of all because of her indomitable people. They are a race of pioneers who have almost beggared themselves to serve others."
—Calvin Coolidge at Bennington on September 21, 1928

While liberal in its politics, Vermonters have proved to be patriotic. In 2007, the state had the highest number of war dead in the Iraqi War, even though three-quarters of residents opposed the war.

Hurricanes are rare in Vermont, but in August 2011, Hurricane Irene slashed its way into the state causing widespread destruction. Nearly every stream and river in the state flooded from the heavy rainfall, and three people died and one went missing. Many of Vermont's famed covered bridges were damaged or destroyed. Repair costs statewide eventually reached up to $200 million.

★ 10 KEY ★ DATES IN STATE HISTORY ★ ★ ★

1. 1609

Samuel de Champlain enters Lake Champlain and claims the land around it, including much of present-day Vermont, for his nation of France. His involvement in a skirmish starts hostilities with the Iroquois that last more than 150 years.

2. 1724

British troops build the first permanent European settlement, called Fort Dummer, to defend Vermont residents from hostile Native American tribes. On October 11, 1724, the Abenaki attack the fort.

3. 1770

Ethan Allen organizes a force of two hundred men called the Green Mountain Boys to protect New Hampshire land grants from New York settlers.

4. January 15, 1777

Vermont declares itself an independent republic, with its own government and constitution.

5. March 4, 1791

Vermont becomes the fourteenth US state, the first to join the union after the original thirteen states.

6. October 19, 1864

Confederate soldiers raid St. Albans during the Civil War, stealing money, damaging property, and terrifying the residents.

7. 1934

The first ski lift in the United States is built in Woodstock by Vermonter Wallace "Bunny" Bertram. It is powered by a Ford Model T engine. In 1937, Pico Peak installs the first T-bar in the US.

8. 1970

Lawmakers pass Act 250, allowing the state to regulate land use based on impact on the environment.

9. January 10, 1985

Madeleine M. Kunin becomes the first female governor of Vermont and the first Jewish woman in any state to become governor. She serves three terms.

10. August 29-30, 2011

Heavy rains from Hurricane Irene cause widespread flooding. Many homes, farms, businesses, roads, and bridges are damaged or destroyed. About a dozen communities are without power or fresh water.

Farming has been a hard but vital way of life in Vermont.

The People

3

More than 625,000 people live in Vermont today. That is a small number compared to most other states. Wyoming is the only state with fewer people. Vermont contains mostly forests, farms, and villages, not big cities. Its heart is in the country, and Vermonters tend to be proud of their ties with the land. They are also known for valuing freedom and independence. Dorothy Canfield Fisher, a well-known Vermont writer and educational reformer, once said there was an unwritten law that every Vermonter "must be allowed to do, think, believe whatever seems best to him."

Vermonters Old and New

About half the people who live in Vermont were born in the state. Many have Vermont roots that go back many generations. Dairy farmer Rosina Wallace still works in the fields bought by her great-grandparents in the 1800s. "Farming is tiring and hard work, but I grew up on this farm," says Wallace. "I love the view almost as much as scratching a cow behind the ears." Other Vermont families have a long tradition of working in granite quarries or lumber mills.

But Vermont has also attracted newcomers from other states. Some were vacationers who decided to stay year-round, perhaps to raise children or enjoy retirement in a

Many newcomers grow organic produce in the state.

comfortable environment. A few started organic farms, raising animals and growing crops without chemical fertilizers or pesticides. Others built businesses selling traditional crafts such as handmade furniture or pottery. Many others found jobs in education, health care, or manufacturing.

People who migrated from other states have become as much a part of Vermont as those whose families lived there for generations. Jay Craven is a filmmaker who moved from New York to Vermont in 1974. He makes movies right near his home in St. Johnsbury and enjoys working with small-town communities. "Vermont has a traditional conservatism," says Craven, "which basically says that for things to change they should change only for good reason. But once the good reason is presented, things do change. There is an openness in Vermont by people to respect all points of view."

Vermont's population hasn't gone through many changes in the last one hundred years. Except for a dip to 314,000 in 1944, the population stayed at close to 360,000 from 1916 to 1960. There was a 50 percent increase in residents in the next forty years, but growth slowed way down in 2000.

Tiny Capital

Montpelier, Vermont's capital city since 1805, has fewer than eight thousand residents. It is by far the smallest capital city in the nation.

The population has remained mostly Caucasian, or white. In fact, according to the 2010 United States Census, Vermont still has a larger proportion of white residents than any other state. Asians and African Americans make up about 2.3 percent of the state's population. Hispanic Americans, who may be of any race, represent about 1.5 percent. Before European settlement, the region's entire population was Native American. Today, however, Native Americans represent only a tiny minority in the state.

Many Vermonters are typical Yankees, tracing their ancestry to the British Isles. These people account for more than one-fourth of the population today. Old Vermont Yankees are assumed to be stubborn and brief in speech with a dry sense of humor. That humor is well displayed in this old Yankee joke: "To New Englanders, a Yankee is a Vermonter. To a Vermonter, a Yankee is someone who eats apple pie for breakfast. And to a Vermonter who eats apple pie for breakfast, a Yankee is someone who eats it with a knife."

Another segment of the population is French Canadian. A good number of them moved from the province of Quebec into mill towns and farms over the border in Vermont during the early 1900s. People of French or French-Canadian descent account for another one-fourth of the current population.

Among other nationalities, around one-fifth of today's Vermonters are Irish. Many of them are descendants of immigrants who came to work on the railroads in the mid-nineteenth century. Large numbers of Vermonters are of German or Italian descent. Others trace their ancestry back to Poland, Scandinavia, the Netherlands, Portugal, or Russia.

In recent years, Vermont has welcomed a greater number of immigrants from Asia, Latin America, and Africa. While these immigrants

Vermont put out the welcome mat to immigrants from Asia and other regions.

10 KEY PEOPLE ★ ★

Ethan Allen

1. Ethan Allen

Born in Connecticut in 1738, Ethan Allen settled in what is now Vermont and organized a militia called the Green Mountain Boys. During the American Revolution, he led his men in taking Fort Ticonderoga in 1775 but was captured in a failed attack on Quebec that same year.

2. Wilson "Snowflake" Bentley

Wilson Bentley, a Vermont farmer, took the first close-up photograph of a snowflake in 1885. "I found that snowflakes were miracles of beauty," he wrote. "Every crystal was a masterpiece of design and no one design was ever repeated."

Keegan Bradley

3. Keegan Bradley

Keegan Bradley of Woodstock was an outstanding ski racer, but he chose to follow his father into golfing. In 2011, he was the PGA Rookie of the Year and won his first major tournament, the PGA Championship.

4. George Dewey

Born in Montpelier, George Dewey commanded the US naval squadron in the Pacific during the Spanish-American War in 1898. He destroyed the Spanish fleet in Manila Bay, the Philippines, without losing an American life.

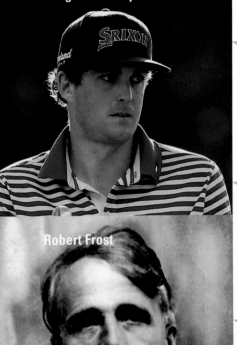
Robert Frost

5. Robert Frost

Born in California in 1874, Robert Frost spent most of his life in New England, where he wrote poetry, taught, and farmed. While living in Vermont, he wrote some of his best-known poems, including "Stopping by Woods on a Snowy Evening."

VERMONT

6. Elisha Otis

Elisha Otis, born in Halifax, was the inventor of the first safety elevator in 1857. As good a businessman as an inventor, Otis manufactured the product in his Otis Elevator Company.

7. Norman Rockwell

Artist Norman Rockwell was born in New York City but lived and worked in Arlington, Vermont, from 1939 to 1953. In his pictures, especially for the covers of the *Saturday Evening Post* and other magazines, he depicted small-town life in loving detail.

8. Patty Sheehan

Born in Middlebury in 1956, Patty Sheehan started concentrating on golf when she was eighteen. She ended up winning five major women's golf championships and was inducted into the World Golf Hall of Fame in 1993.

9. Rudy Vallee

One of the most popular pop singers of his day, Rudy Vallee was born in Island Pond and started his career as a saxophone player. He later led his own band and starred in a number of Hollywood movies and on Broadway.

10. Jody Williams

Born in Brattleboro in 1950, Jody Williams became a leader in the fight against the use of land mines. She co-founded the International Campaign to Ban Landmines (ICBL). In 1997, Williams and the ICBL were awarded the Nobel Peace Prize.

Norman Rockwell

Patty Sheehan

Jody Williams

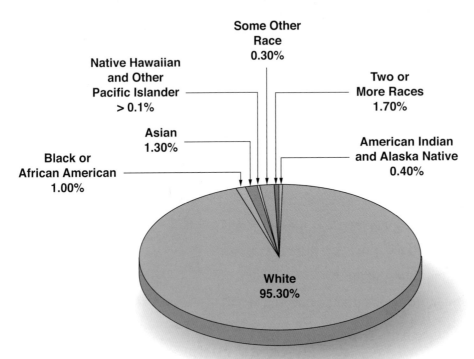

Some Other Race 0.30%

Native Hawaiian and Other Pacific Islander > 0.1%

Two or More Races 1.70%

Asian 1.30%

American Indian and Alaska Native 0.40%

Black or African American 1.00%

White 95.30%

Total Population 625,741

Hispanic or Latino (of any race):
• 9,208 people (1.5%)

Note: The pie chart shows the racial breakdown of the state's population based on the categories used by the US Bureau of the Census. The Census Bureau reports information for Hispanics or Latinos separately, since they may be of any race. Percentages in the pie chart may not add to 100 because of rounding.

Source: US Bureau of the Census, 2010 Census

typically came in search of better opportunity, some were refugees seeking to escape dangerous political situations. For example, a Vermont refugee program that started in 2001 has brought in immigrants from Sudan and Somalia, two African countries torn apart by civil war.

Beginning life over in a new part of the world is often lonely and difficult, but it can also bring hope. Ibrahim Jafar, from Somalia, brought his family to Winooski in 2003. "We knew only that we were going to a strange land, to a place we never heard of, a city we never heard of," he said during a welcome ceremony at Winooski's city hall. "Already it seems like home."

Among the refugees from war-torn areas who built a life in Vermont is this wood carver from Sudan.

Celebrating the Arts

The arts are a big part of life in Vermont. Some of the state's most popular art forms go back to when the state first formed. Others are new and experimental. In a number of Vermont towns, dancers still swing their partners to old-time New England fiddle tunes. People of all ages enjoy what is known as contra dancing. This is a local tradition similar to square dancing except that the couples face each other in rows.

Vermont is an important center for crafts such as woodworking, weaving, pottery, and glassblowing. Many of the artists involved are inspired by traditions. Jeanne Brink makes baskets the way her Abenaki grandmother did long ago, weaving them out of thin strips of wood and grasses. She learned from an older basketmaker, who asked her to promise to keep the craft within the Abenaki people. "I will only teach Abenaki how to make ash-splint and sweet grass baskets," says Brink, "to keep it an Abenaki tradition."

People have been making **quilts** in Vermont since before the American Revolution. A quilter might stitch hundreds of different pieces of cloth together to form a pattern or picture. Quilts that are two hundred years old or more can be found in the Shelburne Museum near Burlington. Historian Richard Cleveland sees them as pieces of the state's past. "Sometimes when I find a quilt I especially like," he says, "I run the tips of my fingers gently over its surface, willing it to tell me its secrets."

Quilters from around the state and around the country come to Essex Junction every June for the Vermont Quilt Festival. It is said to be New England's oldest and largest annual quilt event.

One Vermont group, the Bread and Puppet Theater, took a very old art form and made it into something new. This group was founded in New York City in the 1960s but subsequently relocated to Vermont. Theater members use music, dance, and puppets of all sizes—including figures that tower some 8 feet (2.5 m) high—to entertain, but also to promote the group's own political messages. The Bread and Puppet Theater, which travels during much of the year, presents free outdoor shows in summer on a farm near Glover.

Education

Vermont has about twenty colleges and universities. One of the best-known is the University of Vermont, in Burlington. It is one of the oldest colleges in the United States, dating back to 1791. Now a relatively small, high-ranked public university, it has about fourteen thousand students.

Middlebury College, in the Green Mountains, is a well-respected private liberal arts college with about 2,300 undergraduate students. Many people attend its well-known English and foreign language programs, as well as its Bread Loaf Writers' Conference, which has brought together talented writers and interested students each summer since 1926.

The Vermont constitution of 1777 required each town in the state to have a public school. The state's first secondary, or high, school opened in Bennington in 1780. The first teacher-training school in the nation was established by educator Samuel Read Hall in Concord in 1823.

Vermonters don't stop learning after they finish their schooling. They are avid readers. The state's first library opened in Brookfield in 1791. It remains one of the oldest libraries in the United States still operating. Vermont has more than two hundred public libraries today.

The Rugged Life

One thing nearly all Vermonters have in common is their love for the outdoors. In summer they may head for the Green Mountains to camp, hike, or take a dip in a sparkling lake or clear flowing stream. The Green Mountains' Long Trail is a popular destination for serious hikers. It stretches more than 270 miles (434 km) from the Massachusetts border to Canada. There are convenient campsites along the winding trail every 6 to 8 miles (10 to 13 km). The Green Mountain Club started in 1910 with a goal of building the Long Trail. Now its ten thousand members maintain the Long Trail, the Appalachian Trail, and trails in the Northeast Kingdom (the nickname for the northeast corner of the state).

Almost two-thirds of Vermonters say they like to watch wildlife. That number is more than in any other state. Bird watching is particularly popular. Birders flock to the Nulhegan Basin in the Northeast Kingdom, a wildlife area spanning more than 2,000 square miles (5,180 sq km). On display for birdwatchers are ruffed grouse, black-beaked woodpeckers, and a variety of migratory songbirds.

Fishing is a popular activity. Vermont's clear mountain streams are filled with brook, brown, and rainbow trout. Its lakes and ponds are known for their bass, pike, and walleye. Seyon Lodge State Park features Noyes Pond in the Groton Forest, the only public fly-fishing pond in the state. Ice fishing is popular during the winter months, when lakes and rivers are iced over. The temperature might be below zero, but the reward could be a hefty lake trout, walleye, or northern pike—or just good company. Winter, of course, is also time for skiing, snowboarding, and snowmobiling. There are twenty alpine resorts in the state. Alpine means a place where you can ski or snowboard downhill. Among them are

You can find friendship and fish when ice covers Vermont's lakes and ponds.

world-famous resorts such as Stowe, Smugglers' Notch, and Killington. Killington has the most skiers of any winter sports area east of the Mississippi River, and Ludlow's Okemo Mountain is right behind it.

Jake Burton moved to Vermont and founded Burton Snowboards in 1977. He started by making handmade boards, and then built the first snowboard manufacturing factory in the country. Its headquarters are now in Burlington. He asked around for a place where he and his friends could ride their boards, and in 1983 Stratton Mountain became the first resort in the country to allow snowboarders to use its slopes. The first twenty-seven Burton US Open Snowboarding Championships were held at Stratton Mountain.

Despite Vermont's attractions, everyone who lives there has to face icy winters, muddy springs, and roller-coaster weather. That might be one reason people like to argue about what it takes to be a "real" Vermonter. Some say it means having great-grandparents who were born in the state. To others, it means sticking with the place through thick and thin, even if you come from somewhere else.

The latter was the view of the late Graham Newell, a state senator from a seven-generation Vermont family. "I'm not one of those who says you've got to be born here to be a Vermonter," he once remarked. "If you are a Vermonter, you feel like one and you don't have to explain it."

10 KEY EVENTS ★ ★

New World Festival

Plymouth Cheese and Harvest Festival

1. Abenaki Heritage Weekend

In late June, Native Americans from Vermont and beyond come together in Vergennes to dance, make music, share traditional foods and crafts, and share Abenaki culture with others.

2. Bondville Fair

This fair, held annually near Winhall, is almost as old as the state of Vermont, and it has not changed much over the years. People come every August to eat fried dough, play horseshoes, and see how much weight a team of oxen can pull.

3. Cracker Barrel Bazaar

The highlight of this festive weekend in July is a fiddlers contest on the Newbury Common. Other events include the Cracker Barrel Quest, a scavenger hunt, and a bazaar and craft show.

4. New World Festival

This event, held on Labor Day Sunday in Randolph, celebrates the heritage of traditional Celtic and French American music brought to Vermont by immigrants. In addition to the musical performances, there are puppet shows, dance instruction, and craft displays.

5. Plymouth Cheese and Harvest Festival

This harvest celebration takes place in September at the site of President Calvin Coolidge's family home in Plymouth Notch. Visitors can see what it's like to shear a sheep or play games at home on a farm. They can also tour the cheese factory first opened by Coolidge's father.

VERMONT

6. Stowe Winter Carnival

This winter carnival celebrated its fortieth year in 2014. At this January festival, kids and adults can play snow volleyball, go snowgolfing, watch an ice-carving contest, join a race through the woods on cross-country skis, or take part in a karaoke competition.

7. Vermont Apple Festival

This event over the Columbus Day weekend in Springfield provides activities during the peak of the fall foliage system. There is a farmer's market, a farm animals petting zoo, a bounce house, and an apple pie baking contest.

8. Vermont Dairy Festival

There are lots of events during this dairy farm festival in June in Enosburg Falls. Among other things, visitors can pet prize-winning cows, watch a milking contest, or dance to live country music. Another highlight is the annual 6.2-mile (10 km) "milk run" race.

9. Vermont History Expo

The Vermont Historical Society presents this event every other June at the World's Fair Grounds in Tunbridge. Highlights include historical exhibits, a parade, performances, craft displays, auctions, and other fun activities.

10. Vermont State Fair

The early September event celebrated its 170th year in 2015. Held in Rutland, it is one of the oldest state fairs in the United States. There are agricultural exhibits, pulling contests, harness racing, and musical entertainment.

Stowe Winter Carnival

Vermont State Fair

Soft Serve   Ice Cream
Ice Cream   Cold Drinks

Annual town hall meetings give a
voice to all Vermonters of voting age.

How the Government Works

Ever since the time of the Green Mountain Boys, Vermonters have been ready to fight for what they believe in. They have also been willing to work together to shape Vermont's future. Citizens may come from different backgrounds, but when they speak out and share their ideas, they often find common ground.

Town and County

Close to home, Vermont gives citizens a great way to make their voices heard: the town meeting. There are 237 towns and nine cities in Vermont, and most of them hold such a meeting every year, usually on the first Tuesday in March, which is known as Town Meeting Day across the state. Anyone who is old enough to vote, age eighteen or older, can join in. State law allows any worker the day off to attend a town meeting, and state workers also get the day off.

At town meetings, citizens elect officials, approve budgets, and pass laws. They can also speak out if they disagree with a decision or want to suggest a new law. The town meeting is a New England tradition that goes back to the 1700s. It is often hailed as an outstanding example of democracy at work.

The state's fourteen counties are less important as units of government than are the cities and towns. However, counties do perform certain functions, especially maintaining a system of courts.

Federal and State Government

At the national level, Vermont, like every state big or small, elects two US senators. But, as the second-smallest of the fifty states, Vermont elects only one member to the US House of Representatives, where a state's number of seats is based on its population. Vermont's three federal lawmakers represent the interests of the state and its citizens in Washington, DC. Senators serve six-year terms. Members of the House serve two years. There is no limit on the number of terms a member of Congress can serve.

The Vermont State House in Montpelier was completed in 1859.

The state government is responsible for matters that affect Vermont as a whole. The state has a major role to play in education, transportation, environmental protection, business and economic growth, public health, and public safety. Like the federal government and other state governments, Vermont's government is made up of three branches: executive, legislative, and judicial. Each branch has its own duties and responsibilities.

Branches of Government

Executive

The governor is the state's chief executive officer. He or she runs various departments of the state government and appoints top officials and judges. The governor also can approve or reject proposed laws. Unlike most other states, Vermont elects its governor to two-year terms. (Four-year terms are more common.) A governor can be reelected an unlimited number of times.

Legislative

Vermont's legislature, the General Assembly, is made up of two bodies—the Senate and the House of Representatives. The Senate has thirty members, each of whom represents one or more counties. The House has 150 members, representing about four thousand citizens each. All lawmakers are elected to serve for two years, with no term limits. The legislature meets to hammer out new laws between January and late spring. Most of the members also have other jobs, such as running a business, practicing law, teaching school, or farming.

Judicial

Vermont's highest court is the Supreme Court, headed by a chief justice and also including four associate justices. They serve six-year terms and are appointed by the governor. The supreme court mainly hears appeals of cases decided in lower courts. These include superior courts, for civil cases such as lawsuits, and district courts, for criminal cases. Vermont also has family courts for divorce and child support cases, probate courts for wills, and an environmental court for land use disputes. The Supreme Court has the power to strike down a state law if it judges that the law violates the state constitution.

Most state offices are located in Montpelier, and the state legislature meets in the statehouse there. In addition to being the smallest state capital in the nation, Montpelier is one of the state's smaller cities. Most of its businesses fit on one main street. But its tiny size may be a good thing. It is an easy place for ordinary citizens to meet lawmakers face-to-face.

How a Bill Becomes a Law

The members of Vermont's legislature, or general assembly, make the state's laws. The first step is to put together a proposed law, or bill, and introduce it, or bring it before the state Senate or House of Representatives. Only a member of the legislature can introduce bills, but anyone can suggest a law to a legislator.

After a bill is introduced, it goes to a committee for discussion. Sometimes the committee holds a public hearing, where Vermonters can speak for or against the

In Their Own Words

"We need to provide information to the traveler, but do not want to compromise our natural scenery. Tourism is the number one industry in the state. And the lack of advertising is one of the most commonly repeated things that visitors approve about Vermont."
—John Kessler, chairperson of the Travel Information Council

Bills and budgets are debated in the house chamber of the statehouse.

measure. The committee may reject the bill or support it, either as is or with changes. If and when the committee decides the bill is acceptable, it is read before the whole House or Senate. That is when all members debate the bill and take a vote.

If a bill passes in one house of the general assembly, it then goes to the other, where all these steps have to be repeated. A bill often goes through many changes before the general assembly is done with it.

If all goes smoothly, the bill finally comes to the governor's desk. If the governor signs it, the bill becomes law. But the governor can also **veto**, or reject, a bill. Then it can become law only if two-thirds of both houses vote to "override" the veto. Each year, hundreds of bills are introduced to the general assembly. Out of that number, perhaps one in three eventually becomes a law. To see which bills are going to be introduced or have been passed, visit legislature.vermont.gov and click on Bills & Resolutions.

If you live in Vermont and want to get more involved in determining what happens in the state, the first step is learning more. Find out everything you can by reading various newspapers and

Silly Law

In Barre, it is the law that everyone must bathe on Saturday night.

following the news on the radio, TV, or the Internet. The more you learn about the history of your state and nation and the issues that face people today, the easier it will be to become an informed citizen.

Who Pays for Schools?

One challenge Vermont lawmakers have faced is the divide between rich towns and poor towns. The state's wealthiest communities, sometimes called "gold towns," include skiing centers such as Stratton and Stowe. Most people in these areas have more money and valuable property than citizens in the rest of the state. For a long time, they also had better-funded public schools, because most of the money for schools came from property taxes raised by each town.

In 1997, the Vermont Supreme Court ruled that students throughout the state should have "substantially equal access" to a good education. In response, the state that year passed the Equal Education Opportunity Act, or Act 60. This law, and a further measure that was passed in 2003, set up a complicated system for funding education in the state. In part it required that residents pay property taxes to the state and that the state, through property tax and other **revenues**, provide funding for schools equitably.

Students examine the Vermont constitution, which was written in 1777.

Howard Dean: Governor, 1991-2003

Howard Dean, a liberal Democrat, was the seventy-ninth governor of Vermont. He ran for the Democratic presidential nomination in 2004, becoming a pioneer in Internet campaigning. The following year, he became Chairman of the Democratic National Committee, a post he kept until 2009.

Madeleine Kunin: Governor, 1985-1991

Madeleine Kunin was the first female governor of Vermont and the first Jewish woman to be elected governor of any state. She later served as US ambassador to Switzerland from 1996 to 1999. She now teaches at the University of Vermont.

Patrick Leahy: US Senator, 1975-

The most senior member of the US Senate, Patrick Leahy has long served on the Senate Judiciary Committee. He was its chairman through 2014. He has worked for years on prison reform and has backed much progressive legislation for Vermont. A Batman fan, Leahy has played small roles in several Batman movies.

STATE VERMONT
YOU CAN MAKE A DIFFERENCE

Contacting Lawmakers

To contact a member of the Vermont general assembly, go to

www.leg.state.vt.us/legdir/findmember3.cfm

Using the map, click on your city or town to find your state representative and state senator. If you prefer to pick your city or town by name, click on the text-only version of the page.

Once you know the name of the senator or representative you need, click on "Legislative Directory" and then look for and click on "Representatives Listed Alphabetically" or "Senators Listed Alphabetically." The list contains the information you need to contact your lawmaker by mail, e-mail, or phone.

Sign of Change

Vermont may seem old-fashioned at times, but it has enacted some bold laws, especially related to protecting the environment. Vermont became the first state to outlaw billboards in 1968. But the fight to end billboard blight in the state began decades earlier. In 1937, a citizens committee complained about the placing of seven billboards in Springfield. Soon after people banded

Ted Riehle fought against billboards.

together to form the Vermont Association for Billboard Restriction. Within eighteen months, all seven of the billboards were taken down. Citizens' action groups and garden clubs continued to protest against billboards and the businessmen who wanted them. Through their efforts, an anti-billboard law along limited-access roadways was passed by the Vermont legislature in 1957.

But it wasn't until 1968 that the people found a true champion in a young state legislator and environmental activist, Ted Riehle, who single-handedly led the fight for the first all-state ban on billboards. Riehle later became the state's first planning director and helped set up Vermont's first Green Up Day, an annual event where volunteers clean up the state's roadsides. Riehle later retired to a solar-powered, off-the-grid home on Savage Island in Lake Champlain. He died in 2008.

Vermont's economy has become
increasingly high-tech.

Making a Living

Vermont's fresh air, clear water, and scenery make it a great place to live. It can also be a great place to make a living. Like other states, Vermont was hard hit by the nation's economic downturn that began in late 2007. The unemployment rate, which had been under 4 percent, edged up to more than 7 percent by mid-2009. But this was still below the national average, and conditions showed some improvement in 2010 and the beginning of 2011. By December of 2014, it had fallen all the way to 4.2 percent, which was well below the national average.

The Vermont economy has strengths in many areas. Some people say the state's economy sits on a three-legged stool, being based on manufacturing, agriculture, and tourism. Both manufacturing and agriculture have indeed contributed to the state's growth. But most of the jobs today are in fields that provide services to people, rather than in the production of goods. Tourism, education, health care, and retail trade are among the most common so-called service industries. The state labor commissioner said in early 2015 that the state was seeing an increase in manufacturing jobs, professional services, and health care.

Manufacturing and Mining

Most of Vermont's manufacturing jobs are located near Burlington. Companies in the area make computer chips, software, batteries, and semiconductor equipment. Parts produced in Vermont are needed to make all kinds of electronic items, from video games to cell phones. The state's high-tech industries have become increasingly important to Vermont's economy.

With its millions of acres (hectares) of forests, Vermont also remains a center for wood and paper products. Sawmills produce lumber, cabinetmakers build furniture, and printing presses turn out newspapers and business forms. Some companies in the state make equipment for outdoor sports, including snowboards, snowshoes, and fishing rods.

Textile manufacturing declined in the twentieth century as cotton textile factories moved south and synthetic fabrics came into wide use. Machine tools, for use in factories, fared better. Some of the first tools for shaping wood and metal by machine were invented in Windsor in the 1840s. These tools were used to make guns, typewriters, and sewing machines in the state. Today, machine tools made in Vermont help produce paper, steel, cars, and airplanes in factories across the country.

The country's first granite quarry lies just outside Barre, on the eastern side of the Green Mountains. Workers cut big blocks of the rock and haul them to workshops called granite sheds. Some chunks of Vermont granite are carved and polished to make memorial stones. Others are sliced to make the walls of office buildings or cut up for use as kitchen countertops.

Marble has long been one of Vermont's most important exports.

Vermont's marble belt runs through the Taconic Mountains, in the southwestern part of the state. For more than one hundred years, stonecutters in Proctor have been shaping marble columns and graceful monuments. The United Nations Building in New York City is made from Vermont marble. So are the US Supreme Court Building and the Jefferson Memorial in Washington, DC.

Today, most of this gleaming white stone is ground into a fine powder called calcium carbonate. It is then used to make toothpaste, paint, and plastics.

Living from the Land

Green fields, red barns, and black-and-white cows are a familiar sight in Vermont. Farming is no longer the state's key industry, but even today some seven thousand farms dot the landscape and make an important contribution to the economy. Despite the rocky soil and less-than-ideal climate conditions, Vermont farmers still make a living growing fruits and vegetables, such as apples and potatoes, as well as crops for animal feed, such as hay, corn, oats, and wheat. Some farmers use greenhouses to raise warm-weather produce such as green peppers and tomatoes, as well as nursery plants.

Dairy products, however, are the most important farm resource, accounting for two-thirds of all farm revenue. Dairy farms blanket the Lake Champlain valley. Some have been around for more than two hundred years, with the oldest dating back to the American Revolution. At one time, Vermont had more cows than people. Today there are

Vermont is the country's leader in all things maple.

10 KEY INDUSTRIES

Apples

Electronic Goods

1. Apples

The state has some 3,200 acres (1,300 ha) of commercial apple orchards. Crisp Vermont apples are either sold fresh or made into products such as cider, applesauce, and pie. From mid-August through October, families can visit many of the state's orchards and enjoy apple picking together.

2. Electronic Goods

Electronics is Vermont's leading manufacturing industry, and the International Business Machines Corporation, better known as IBM, is the state's biggest employer. The IBM semiconductor plant near Burlington is the biggest industrial plant in the state.

3. Fancy Food and Drink Products

Vermont is home to some best-selling artisan foods, including Cabot Cheese, Vermont Butter and Cheese Company, and Lake Champlain Chocolate, that sell locally and ship their products around the world. The state has a number of microbrewies and at least fifteen wineries.

4. Forests

The 4.46 million acres (17.9 million ha) of trees that carpet Vermont make up 78 percent of the state's land. The trees are used to make everything from lumber to firewood to maple syrup. Their fiery fall color attracts tourists.

5. Granite

Some of the world's finest granite comes from quarries near Barre, where this stone is an important part of the economy. Vermont ships this heavy building material across the United States and to many other countries.

VERMONT

6. Milk

Some 135,000 Vermont dairy cows help make milk an important state product. The most common type are black-and-white Holsteins. Each cow can provide more than 6 gallons (23 l) of milk a day.

7. More Minerals

Granite is not Vermont's only major mined mineral. Vermont is a leading producer of asbestos, marble, slate, and talc. Sand, gravel and limestone are also mined in Vermont.

8. Mountains and Snow

Vermont's mountains attract hikers, campers, and sightseers. In 2013–2014, Vermont was ranked number one in the East and number three in the United States in skiing and snowboarding visits.

Mountains and Snow

9. Paper and Paper Products

Manufacturing paper and paper products is the number one wood-processing industry in the state. Paper mills throughout Vermont turn wood pulp into paper used to produce newspapers, stationary, magazines, cardboard, and other paper products.

10. Tourism

Millions of visitors travel to Vermont each year, bringing money to the state economy. In summer, people come to hike, camp, fish, and swim in rivers and lakes. In autumn, tourists come especially to enjoy the brilliant fall leaves. Tourists help keep the economy running by staying at hotels, eating in restaurants, and shopping in stores.

Tourism

Recipe for Sugar on Snow

Sugar on snow is a longtime Vermont tradition. Among farming families, the first day's maple syrup boiling is often celebrated with this dessert treat. Here is a simple recipe for it.

What You Need

Pure maple syrup, ¼ cup
(59 milliliters) per person

Clean snow from right after a snowfall,
or finely crushed ice will do

Small serving bowls

A cooking pan

A candy thermometer

What to Do

- Pour the maple syrup into the pan and have an adult help you heat the pan on the stove to about 20 degrees above the boiling point of water, which is 212 degrees Farenheit (100 degrees Celsius). Test it with the thermometer until the temperature reaches 234°F (112°C). Then let the syrup cool a bit in the pan.

- Put the snow or crushed ice into the bowls and spoon a tablespoon of the syrup over one as a test. The syrup should sit on top of the snow. If it clings to a fork the way taffy does, it's ready to eat.

- Pour the syrup over each bowl, peel it off the ice, and then dig in.

- If you really want to have a sugar on snow party like Vermonters do, serve sour pickles and plain doughnuts with your dessert.

fewer cows, but they actually produce more milk, around 2.5 billion pounds (1.1 billion kg) per year. More than half of it is shipped to other states, while a small amount is sold locally for drinking. The rest goes to make dairy products such as yogurt, butter, ice cream, and more than fifteen kinds of cheese, especially cheddar and mozzarella.

Many farmers earn money from a famous Vermont resource: the sweet sap of the sugar maple tree. They tap the trees by driving a metal spout into the trunk and letting the sap drip into a metal bucket. Pipeline systems are also used to collect the sap. Then, the farmers boil the sap down to make syrup or mouthwatering maple sugar candy. Vermont is the leading maple product producer among the fifty states. Maple products alone account for about 6 percent of the state's farm revenue.

Ice Cream

One of the best-known Vermont products is Ben & Jerry's premium ice cream. In 1978, two friends, Ben Cohen and Jerry Greenfield, went into business together so they could be their own bosses—and have fun. They made their own ice cream and sold it in a run-down former gas station in Burlington. Today, people buy their many flavors around the world. As the company grew, Ben and Jerry made sure some of the profits went to causes they believed in. While their ice cream is still a big hit, Ben and Jerry sold the company in 2000 and are no longer involved in running it.

Tourism

Millions of visitors travel to Vermont each year, bringing money to the state economy. In summer, people come to hike and camp in untamed areas, such as the Green Mountain National Forest, and to swim, fish, and canoe in sparkling rivers and lakes. In autumn, tourists come especially to enjoy the brilliant fall leaves. Winter brings skiers and snowboarders to mountain resorts such as Stowe, Smugglers' Notch, Killington, and Sugarbush.

In addition, many people from outside Vermont have vacation homes in the state. These part-time Vermonters buy property and also pay taxes, giving the state a financial boost.

The outdoors may be Vermont's main tourist attraction, but history and the arts bring people to the state, too. The Shelburne Museum, just south of Burlington, is not just one building, but almost fifty, spread out in a huge park with green lawns and bright flowers. Many of the buildings are more than a century old, including a schoolhouse from 1840 and an inn from 1783. Inside them is one of the largest collections of arts and crafts from America's past.

Art and woodwork are features of the Shelburne Museum.

Saving Vermont Farms

Many visitors like to come to Vermont for its simple pleasures. Tourists can drive along a narrow, winding road, pass a two-hundred-year-old covered bridge, buy fresh fruit from a farmer, and then browse in a country store. Vermonters hope the state will be able to keep its old-fashioned charm for years to come. That means protecting the land and preserving historic places. It also means holding on to an important part of the rural way of life: Vermont's farms.

Farming has never been an easy job, and soil and weather conditions in Vermont are tougher than in many other states. Prices can drop so low that farmers earn less money than they need to pay out for feed, equipment, and property taxes. Owners of small farms have an especially hard time. Nowadays farmers often wind up selling their land to developers, who will pay a high price for the land and use it to build houses or businesses.

Most farmers would rather keep their land if they can still make it profitable, and other people want them to keep it too. "Vermont wouldn't be Vermont without its farmers," says Pam Allen, who grows apples on an old family farm in South Hero. "People here don't want to see parking lots and high-rises. There is no other sight in the world like these apple trees exploding with sweet white blossoms each spring."

Vermonters are doing their best to keep small farms running. They are looking for a cheaper way to produce "organic" milk (produced without the use of chemicals) so they can sell it at a good profit. Other farmers are switching to organic crops. People will pay more for organic products, but these also cost more to produce. Some farmers run inns for tourists who are looking to enjoy the experience of life on a farm. Others make and sell specialty foods such as gourmet mushrooms and homestyle jam.

Conservation groups are helping out. The Vermont Land Trust, for example, pays farmers who agree to protect their land from development. Since the group got started in the 1970s, it has saved more than 500,000 acres (200,000 ha) in the state, including 750 working farms. Another organization, the Conservation Law Foundation, is working with the state government to get help for farmers, including tax relief, business advice, and programs to promote products that are grown close to home. One such program, called Vermont Fresh Network, links farmers to restaurants interested in buying their crops.

Farms contribute hundreds of millions of dollars a year to the Vermont economy. They also create the green rolling pastures the state is famous for. Vermonters hope to preserve this valuable asset.

State Mineral

Vermont is the second leading producer of talc, the state mineral, in the United States. Only California produces more of it. One of the softest minerals, talc is crushed to make talcum powder, a great absorber of moisture.

Vermonters work to preserve their farms.

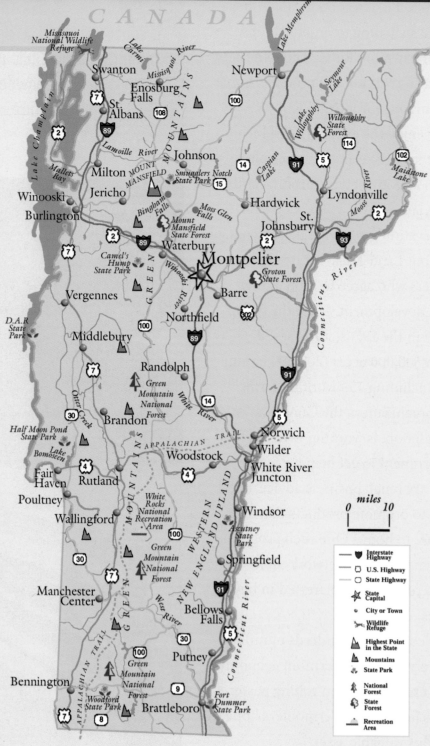

CANADA

Missisquoi National Wildlife Refuge

Lake Carmi

Lake Memphremagog

Swanton

Missisquoi River

Newport

Seymour Lake

Enosburg Falls

(100)

St. Albans

7

(108)

Lake Willoughby

Willoughby State Forest

114

89

Lamoille River

Johnson

(14)

Caspian Lake

91

5

Lake Champlain

Milton

MOUNT MANSFIELD

Smugglers Notch State Park

15

102

Maidstone Lake

Mallets Bay

Jericho

Bingham Falls

Mount Mansfield State Forest

Moss Glen Falls

Hardwick

Lyndonville

Winooski

St. Johnsbury

Moose River

2

Burlington

GREEN

Waterbury

2

93

2

89

Camel's Hump State Park

Montpelier

Groton State Forest

Connecticut River

7

Winooski River

Barre

Vergennes

Northfield

(302)

D.A.R State Park

(100)

89

91

Middlebury

Randolph

Green Mountain National Forest

White River

(14)

Otter Creek

5

Brandon

Norwich

Half Moon Pond State Park

APPALACHIAN TRAIL

Wilder

Lake Bomoseen

Woodstock

White River Junction

4

Fair Haven

Rutland

4

White Rocks National Recreation Area

Windsor

Poultney

WESTERN

Ascutney State Park

Wallingford

(100)

(30)

Green Mountain National Forest

NEW ENGLAND UPLAND

Springfield

7

91

Manchester Center

MOUNTAINS

GREEN

West River

Bellows Falls

(100)

(30)

5

Putney

Bennington

Green Mountain National Forest

9

APPALACHIAN TRAIL

Woodford State Park

Brattleboro

Fort Dummer State Park

7

8

miles
0   10

Interstate Highway	
U.S. Highway	
State Highway	
State Capital	
City or Town	
Wildlife Refuge	
Highest Point in the State	
Mountains	
State Park	
National Forest	
State Forest	
Recreation Area	

VERMONT ★ ★ ★
MAP SKILLS

1. What body of water is Winooski located on?

2. What recreational area is located in south central Vermont?

3. What is the capital city of Vermont?

4. What town is located directly west from Rutland along Route 4?

5. What interstate highway parallels the Connecticut River?

6. What is the highest point in the state?

7. What is the most southerly city in Vermont?

8. What mountain range crosses the central part of the state from north to south?

9. What state road passes through Wallingford, Rutland, and Middlebury?

10. What wildlife refuge is on the Vermont-Canadian border?

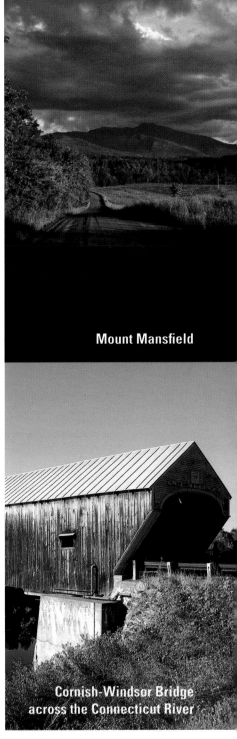

Mount Mansfield

Cornish-Windsor Bridge across the Connecticut River

10. Missisquoi National Wildlife Refuge
9. Route 7
8. The Green Mountains
7. Brattleboro
6. Mount Mansfield
5. Interstate 91
4. Fair Haven
3. Montpelier
2. White Rocks National Recreational Area
1. Lake Champlain

State Flag, Seal, and Song

Vermont's flag was adopted in 1923. It displays the state's coat of arms against a blue background. The coat of arms includes a shield with symbols of the state's forests and farms: a pine tree, a cow, bales of hay, and stacks of wheat, with the Green Mountains in the background. The head of a stag, or male deer, is shown at the top of the shield, and pine branches curve around it. The name of the state and Vermont's motto, "Freedom and Unity," appear on a red banner underneath.

The official state seal was created by Ira Allen, an early settler who, like his brother Ethan, helped Vermont become a state. The seal was originally adopted in 1779. It shows the state motto below a pine tree, a cow, sheaves of grain, and wooded hills. A newer version was introduced in 1821, but in 1937, Vermonters decided to return to Ira Allen's original design.

"These Green Mountains" was made the state song in 2000, replacing "Hail to Vermont." The people of Vermont helped to choose the song in a competition. The words and music were written by Diane Martin.

To hear the song, visit: **www.50states.com/songs/vermont.htm#.Vln58slqlvk**

Glossary

agriculture	The science or occupation of farming.
algae	Plantlike organisms that live in water and have no roots.
constitution	A set of laws by which a country or government is run.
deciduous	Trees that shed leaves each year.
economy	The management of a country's or state's resources.
glaciers	Slow-moving masses of ice.
immigrants	People who leave their homeland to live in another country.
legislators	Elected persons who make laws for a state or country.
militia	A body of citizens who become soldiers for a temporary period of time.
predators	Animals that kill and eat other animals.
quarry	An open pit from which building stone or minerals are taken out.
quilts	Kinds of blankets made from two layers of fabric with a soft filler in between.
revenues	The total collected income by a state, country, or business.
rural	Pertaining to country life or country people.
veto	A refusal by an executive, such as a governor, to sign a bill passed by a legislature so it becomes a law.
wigwam	A dome-shaped hut with a wooden frame that is covered with animal skin or tree bark.

More About Vermont

BOOKS

Boekhoff, P. M. *Ben and Jerry*. Detroit: KidHaven Press, 2005.

Bushnell, Mark. *It Happened in Vermont*. It Happened In Series. Guilford, CT: Globe Pequot Press, 2009.

Haugen, Brenda. *Ethan Allen: Green Mountain Rebel*. Minneapolis: Compass Point Books, 2005.

Sommers, Michael. *Vermont Past and Present*. New York: Rosen Publishing Group, 2010.

Venezia, Mike. *Calvin Coolidge*. Danbury, CT: Children's Press, 2007.

Wooten, Sarah McIntosh. *Robert Frost: The Life of America's Poet*. Berkeley Heights, NJ: Enslow Publishers, 2006.

WEBSITE

Official State of Vermont Tourism Site
www. vermontvacation.com

ABOUT THE AUTHORS

Margaret Dornfield is a writer, editor, and translator in New York City. She enjoys canoeing on the lakes and rivers of Vermont.

William McGeveran, the former editorial director at World Almanac Books, is a freelance editor and writer.

Steven Otfinoski has written more than 160 books for young readers, including many state books. He lives in Connecticut and has spent many happy weekends in Vermont.

Index

Index